Veni
the ISLANDS of the LAGOON

Pearls of land forgotten in the sea

arsenale editrice

Editorial co-ordination
Arsenale Editore

Text
Giovanni Cavarzere

Photography
Archivio Arsenale

English translation
Peter Eustace

Venice
the Islands of the Lagoon
Pearls of land forgotten in the sea

First Edition January 2009

© ARSENALE EDITRICE

Arsenale Editore Srl
Via Ca' Nova Zampieri, 29
37057 - San Giovanni Lupatoto (Verona)
Italy

Introduction

Venice is often imagined only to be the island of the Rialto and St. Mark's - and in fact, by now, it is hardly ever thought to be island as such, following the construction of the Freedom Causeway by the Austrians in the mid-1800s linking it with firm land. In reality, while Venice was the capital of a vast maritime empire, the islands surrounding it were a natural extension, where highly important economic, religious and social activities took place. The famous Murano glass-works were transferred to this island to prevent fires in Venice itself and the economic return was so important that the Serene Republic in fact prohibited glass-workers against travelling abroad. Some of the islands in the lagoon were also used to welcome the many pilgrims travelling to the Holy Land, foreigners seeking passage on Venetian ships against payment, while many others were home to convents and monasteries. The first monks to settle in the lagoon were the Benedectines, who subsequently developed very strong bonds with the Republic of St. Mark, so much so that it was in their church of San Nicolò del Lido that the doge celebrated the "sea wedding" ceremony. In some cases, the islands were used to quarantine goods and people from distant lands, rich in spices but also carriers of terrible diseases, and it was precisely in the Veneto lagoon that the first leper colony in history was founded. The dune islands such as Lido and Pellestrina were also the natural barrier that separated the lagoon from the open sea, protecting it against the worst storms, and also serving as a defensive bastion. After the fall of the Serene Republic, the umbilical cord that linked Venice with its satellites was cut and the only important function given to many of them by the French and the Austrians was entirely military: convents and churches were demolished and their place was taken by munitions depots and defensive batteries. Later, during the Kingdom of Italy, the particular characteristics of certain islands were exploited - in other words, their isolation - to build hospitals and sanatoriums for patients suffering from contagious diseases, yet in the 1970-80s military and health functions alike came to an end and the smaller islands were abandoned and neglected. By the end of the 1990s, however, work to recover these islands became a priority objective of institutions - and in some cases this is already a reality, thanks not the least to the involvement of private-sector companies. This book by no means seeks to provide a complete history of the lagoon islands but simply aims to highlight some salient aspects, saving them from the shadows where the marvels of Venice are all too often hidden away.

 Burano

Famous for its highly colourful homes, Burano is extremely charming and for this reason nicknamed the "Harlequin island". Strolling along its alleys and canals is a feast for the eyes and the people of Burano are so proud of the beauty of their homes that the plasterwork is repainted every year. Like Murano, Burano also takes its name from that of an Altino gate - the Boreana Gate - and is famed all over the world not only for its colours: here, the 1500s saw the development of superb lace-work, envied by all European nobility; even the ministers of Louis XIV, in the high mercantile times, made strenuous efforts to persuade the skilled craftsmen of Burano to settle in France with promises of wealth and fortunate marriages. Today, we can still admire the finest and most precious creations in the Lace Museum, overlooking the main square, where there is also the School that still today promotes and encourages the art of lace embroidery among new generations. The island was originally a suburb of the more important island of Torcello but, when the northern part of the lagoon was swamped by rivers, Burano was spared by favourable currents that helped keep it healthy. Torcello and the other islands were therefore abandoned, while Burano continued to prosper, especially thanks to fishery: still today there is no family without a boat, as evident in the busy canals, and its inhabitants are considered to be skilled fishermen and the only true experts of the secrets of the northern lagoon.

Burano: bottom left, the church of San Martino.
The adjacent bell tower is a smaller copy of St. Mark's.
Top right, the bridge with Mazzorbo.

Burano: a characteristic view. The island is famous for its brightly painted houses.

 Certosa

Certosa is an example of how islands in the lagoon left to vandals and deterioration can be revitalised. There were originally two islands but in 1199 the canal separating them was filled in and a church dedicated to St. Andrew and a monastery of Augustinian Fathers were built. In the 1400s, the Augustinians were replaced by the Carthusians, who commissioned Pietro Lombardo to build a splendid church embellished with works by great masters such as Tintoretto, Palma the Young, Titian and Vivarini. The monks upheld the rules of their order by each living in small, individual cells, all with a well and a small garden, where they were buried at the end of their earthly lives. The monastery and the adjacent church received generous donations from many noble families, who built here their family tombs. In 1806, the suppression of the convents and the expropriation of ecclesiastical assets saw extensive sacking of the works of art in the complex, but the decision to build the city cemetery at San Michele finally decreed the end of the Certosa. The two islands were both candidates as the home to this cemetery: San Michele was chosen and retained its magnificent church, while the Certosa was demolished - perhaps the most devastating event of its kind in the history of art. Thereafter, the island was granted to military authorities by all the subsequent City Councils of Venice. Ultimately, the Italian Army installed a factory producing explosives, which was only closed in 1958, and a light-weapon test range that was active until 1968. After closure, the Certosa was abandoned and became overgrown by wild and uncontrollable vegetation, while the military stopped all upkeep. In the early 1990s, Venice City Council, together with the *New Venice Consortium* and the Water Magistracy, began reclamation and restoration work that saw the renaissance of the island. Since 2004, the island has been home to *Wind of Venice*, a multi-purpose nautical centre: activities include the construction of hulls, a sailing school, charter hire and rental of facilities for conventions and ceremonies.

I Lazzaretti

A city such as Venice, whose prosperity was founded on maritime trade, had to face the dire problem of pestilence: how could plagues be controlled without halting trade? In 1428, the Senate adopted a suggestion of St. Bernard of Siena and converted the island of Santa Maria of Nazareth into a place where peo-

Lazzaretto Vecchio and its characteristic trapezoidal shape.

ple and goods from infected countries could be quarantined. This was the first "lazzaretto" (leper colony) in history and took its name from a distortion of Nazareth, turning it from "Nazareto" into "Lazareto". In 1468, another island – Vinea Murata – was converted into a place of quarantine and named "Lazzaretto Nuovo" and in 1564 the "Lazzaretto Vecchio" was extended by filling in a part of the surrounding lagoon. While "Lazzaretto Vecchio" was home to evident sufferers, the new site was used to quarantine people and goods from places considered to be at risk: the large vineyard planted by the friars of San Giorgio Maggiore progressively gave way to small new homes and large depots for goods. These islands were subject to a very strict rule to ensure their isolation: relatives and friends could not tie up their boats but only approach within shouting distance. The boats used to carry food and water to the "lazzaretti" were checked by soldiers stationed on the islands, so that no one could leave and anyone attempting to escape was hung from the gallows located in a very prominent place. Goods were stored in huge sheds: The 1500s *Tezon Grando*, built at "Lazzaretto Nuovo", was the largest Venetian building after the rope yards at the Arsenal. They were roofed buildings with huge windows, since it was believed that the plague was propagated by unhealthy air and that a continual

Lido: *Foreground, the Alberoni octagon, built in the 1500s by the Serene Republic for defensive purposes. Today it is a private home. Background, Lido island and the port inlets.*

current would purify the goods. Goods were also subjected to fumigations with pyrethrum and other medicinal plants; the same treatment was used for the post addressed to the "guests" of the island, which was then delivered to them by servants using a long pole to avoid direct contact. During the huge epidemic in 1576, the two "lazzaretti" no longer sufficed to house all actual and suspected sufferers, and thousands of boats of all kinds, crowded with victims, formed a kind of crown around the two islands resembling a kind of siege by the living dead. Progress in medicine saw the end of these colonies and, between the end of the 1700s and the start of the next century, the two islands became military centres – that in turn saw inevitable demolitions and the building of landfills, barracks and defensive walls. *Tezon Grando* remained standing and the huge windows were walled up to turn it into a powderhouse. Once their defensive function also came to an end, the two "lazzaretti" took different roads: the "Old" site, like so many other smaller islands, was abandoned and neglected – yet work began in 2004 to create the Venice Lagoon Archaeological Museum, a project costing €25 million that should be completed in 2010; the "New" site, on the other hand, was granted under concession by public authorities to Ekos Club, an association of volunteers, and has enjoyed a new life for many years. The association hosts the Summer Camps of the Archeo Club, that have brought to light finds dating back to the Roman age that are now collected in a museum. Restoration of the walls and defensive works – of *Tezon Grando* and other buildings – by the Superintendency and the Water Magistracy have turned them all into a precious jewel.

Il Lido

Together with Pellestrina, it is one of the two islands forming the barrier between the lagoon and the open sea; they are both made up of sandy detritus carried by the rivers flowing out into the lagoon that were later deviated by the Serene Republic to prevent silting. Until the 1800s, the Lido was almost deserted but the invention of seaside resorts and the sun-tan fashion saw very swift development. The first resort was built at Malamocco – in Roman times a trading post for the city of Padua and from v century a safe refuge for hundreds of people escaping the fury of the Huns. In 742, Malamocco became the home of the doge, and thus the most important centre of the lagoon; nevertheless, the doges and city administration were transferred in 811 for better safety to the Rialto islands, where Venice then rose. This transfer initiated its decline, so much so that by the early XII century Malamocco disappeared in quite unclear circumstances, as if it had sunk into the abyss like Atlantis. What we know today as Malamocco is a township set up much later; yet it was only in 1339 that it earned a "podestà" or governor, who also had jurisdiction over Pellestrina. Apart from this village, the island was only home to the Benedictine convent of San Nicolò, at the northern tip. The same site later saw the construction of the fortress of the same name to prevent enemy ships entering the lagoon, together with the Sant'Andrea fort on Vignole island. In the mid-1800s, sea-side resorts turned the Lido from a forgotten agricultural outpost into a meeting place for the international jet set. The *Belle Epoque* was its most flourishing period: the resorts were extended to welcome wealthy holiday-makers from all over Europe and many important buildings in the *Liberty* style were erected. The Great War saw the San Nicolò fort turned into the Navy High Command, with the inevitable decline of the resorts that continued through to the end of the conflict. In the 1930s, it was decided to revitalise the area as the summer home of Venice Casino – as is still the case today – and especially by turning it into the home for the Cinema Festival. The result was long-lasting but at the same time focuses almost exclusively on this event: high society invades the island during the Exhibition Week, only to forget it for the rest of the year. After the Second World War, the Lido became the residential centre of Venice and witnessed rapid building development. Its ancient, wild nature is only recalled at the southernmost tip, where Alberoni still has a partly free sand-dune beach – but also an exclusive golf course. Here, we can still admire the intact Alberoni Octagon, a fortress built in the 1500s on a tiny artificial island as part of the defensive system designed by the Serene Republic to protect its ports.

La Giudecca

Once called Spinalonga, probably after its elongated shape resembling a backbone, Giudecca is usually considered to be an integral part of Venice. In reality, the island was always a separate place precisely because the Venetians wanted to keep it distinct from the rest of the city. Its name derives from Zudecà, which in Venetian dialect means "judged": in IX century, in short, the lands of the island were granted to several families in recompense for unfair

The monumental facade of the Redentore Church, on Giudecca island.

exile. Later, and until the 1500s, the island was widened and lengthened through a series of consolidation and reclamation works and the new land allowed monasteries and aristocratic villas to be built. Thanks to such buildings, Giudecca took on physiognomy quite different to rest of Venice: the monks and the noble families alike, in short, hoped to obtain in their new homes what they could not have in Venice itself: orchards and gardens. This saw the appearance of quiet monasteries and even country villas with huge parks and gardens crowded by festive people in Summer. A few oar-strokes took people far away from the hubbub of the city to complete peace and quiet. This may seem impossible for anyone now looking at this island from the city, given the endless row of palaces and houses enclosing the view, but behind them there were once botanical gardens with exotic plants and well-tended parks. Today, as then, everything is dominated by the Redentore Church, built to a design by Andrea Palladio in thanks for the end of the terrible plague in 1576. The beams of the refectory were prepared by dismantling some of the ships that took part in the victory at the Battle of Lepanto (1571). With the end of the Serene Republic, the nobility lost the privileges that allowed them to maintain such costly villas and the monasteries were closed following the suppression of numerous religious orders. In many cases, the land was left untilled and several convents were demolished - yet the island continued in other ways to retain its own distinct identity: no longer gardens for pleasant pass-times but factories, shipyards, prisons and barracks. Anything the Venetians did not want was shifted to Giudecca that in this way, however, retained its precise physiognomy. The closure of the stone workshops (that were even once home to a brewery!) caused a period of deterioration, although many of these abandoned places have since seen fine restoration. One of the most impressive it the Stucky Mill, an imposing neo-gothic brick building designed by German architect Ernest Wullekopft and built in 1896. This industrial complex was immediately and severely criticised, given its northern European style little suited to the Venetian context, yet perhaps it is precisely such unusualness that makes it so fascinating. The mill involved avant-garde technical solutions, employed 1,500 people and processed 2,500 quintals of flour/day. The intuition that inspired the founder – Giovanni Stucky – was based on the speed of transport by water compared to land and was very successful until Stucky was murdered by an employee in 1910: his son Giancarlo was unable to combat the competition, in the wake of new roads and railways, and after slow by continual decline this mill was closed in 1954. In 1988, it became a listed historic-artistic building and the 1990s saw the onset of complex and difficult restoration work, that was only completed at the end of May 2007. Today, the Mill is a luxury hotel complex boasting a congress centre with two thousand places and a residential area.

La Grazia

La Grazia is almost a compendium of everything that an island in the lagoon could have become over the centuries: shoal, inn, convent, military site and then a hospital … it is almost like tracing the history of the lagoon in miniature.

Known in ancient times as Santa Maria delle Grazie, it was also called Cavana or Cavanella since, after its concession in the X century to the monks of San Giorgio, it was the only shoal offering refuge to boats and ships taken by surprise by lagoon storms. Such continual silting turned it into a small island and by 1264 an inn especially welcomed English, German and French pilgrims travelling to the Holy Land. In the 1400s, it became home to a convent of the monks of San Girolamo da Fiesole, who built a fine monastery here with a cloister boasting as many as forty columns, while the church itself had canvases by Tintoretto, Veronese and Longhi. In 1412, a merchant brought here from Byzantium an icon of the Virgin as a votary gift for grace received and this episode gave the island its name. At the end of the 1600s, the monastic order was suppressed by the Pope and all its assets were given to the Serene Republic. A few years later, the convent was occupied by Capuchin nuns only to see the definitive suppression of the monastery by Napoleon and in 1810 the complex, including the church, was demolished to make way for a powder-house. It was blown up in 1849 during the Risorgimento revolts and it was only in the early 1900s that the site came to be used as a hospital for patients suffering from contagious diseases. In 1952, a new ward was built for polio victims and physical rehabilitation. Today, La Grazia is totally neglected – although the Venice Health Authority (which owns the site) has recently issued a tender to sell it to private investors capable of valorising it.

The apse of the Romanesque Basilica of San Donato in Murano.

Mazzorbo

Human settlements on the island date back to Roman times, as indicated by its name derived from the Latin *Majurbium*; like other islands in this part of the lagoon, it is was swamped and progressively abandoned. Today, it is linked by a bridge to nearby Burano but its appearance is entirely different: here, instead of alleys and canals, there are vegetable gardens and orchards, with occasional remains of 1400s villas reflected in the water. The ancient and numerous churches and

monasteries are only witnessed by the leaning bell tower of the church of Santa Maria in Valverde and the church of Santa Caterina. Like many other lagoon hermitages, Mazzorbo was famed for the easy-going character of its nuns, always willing to offer warm hospitality to guests, especially after the abandonment of the Bishop's See in Torcello and the consequent lack of vigilance by religious authorities. Today, it resembles open countryside, yet where we now see rows of fruit trees for centuries there were houses, alleys, shops and squares. There is still a small village, close to the bridge with Burano.

Murano

Crossed by a Grand Canal in miniature, like other lagoon islands Murano also owes its name to one of the Altino Gates - Ammurianum: the Altino people in v century had to seek refuge here and on other islands to escape the warring Huns, who were skilful horse-riders but disastrous sailors. Famous all over the world for its glass work, Murano is also

Murano: *the island divided its own the Grand Canal. Famous for its glassworks, until the end of the 1500s it was home to feasts and wild nights for nobles arriving in Summer by brightly-lit gondolas.*

known as the "fire island" because of the many furnaces that still today characterise this island. The origin of this fundamental characteristic is the outcome of a strict law imposed by the Serene Republic: in 1292, the Lords of Venice decreed that all the furnaces in Venice should be transferred to Murano, to avoid the disastrous consequences of fires (Venice at the time was a city largely built with wood). The island had already enjoyed administrative autonomy for some time, had its own "podestà" (governor) and a council with law-making powers. Murano also had its own currency – the "Osella" – although in reality it was not freely exchanged. In ancient times, the doge donated five "oselle" every year to each of the noble families, that is five wild ducks. In 1571, it was decided for practical reasons to turn this into a symbolic gift by minting coins named after the ancient tradition: by then, there were 500 nobles in Murano and hunting 2500 ducks had become far too complicated and risked the extinction of the species! In this period, the island saw the construction of sumptuous palaces by noble families as "second homes" for relaxation and receptions. Summer nights often saw long processions of well-lit gondolas leave Venice carrying endless numbers of aristocrats to the feasts in Murano. The glass-works exported their precious artefacts all over the world. This business was so important that Venice had forbidden glass workers to emigrate in its concern that its monopoly would become common knowledge. Every glass-works in Murano had its own secret recipe: every master glass-worker had personal recipes to give glass a particular colour. Some master craftsmen kept their catalogues up-to-date and stayed ahead of the competition even by employing trusted alchemists. These forerunners of chemistry were allowed free use of laboratories in the glassworks to conduct their experiments and in exchange provided formulas to give glass new and extraordinary colours. When the aristocracy turned its attention to the hinterland and began building their sumptuous country villas, Murano lost its characteristic "brio" – and chinaware and crystal glass from Bohemia did the rest: the island progressively declined. Noble palaces were even demolished in order to re-use their materials. In the 1800s, the French closed and demolished numerous churches and convents on the island, yet the beauty of the Romanesque Church of San Donato can still be admired.

Poveglia

A very ancient trading point linked with Padua, its Latin name *Popilia* was inspired by its numerous poplars. In v century, it was inhabited by exiles from the hinterland seeking refuge from the barbarian hordes. Three centuries later, Pipin and his Franks unsuccessfully attempted to capture Venice and the people of Poveglia followed the footsteps of their ancestors: they fled from the barbarian invaders and left the island deserted. In 864, doge Pietro Tradonico was assassinated for his despotism and his followers barricaded themselves in the Ducal Palace. The new doge, Orso I Partecipazio, settled the situation by donating Poveglia to the rebels and at the same time exempted them from military service and payment of taxes. They were also granted the privilege of mooring their boats at Bucintoro during the Sensa Feast and the following Sunday the doge had to hold a banquet for them, during which they could kiss his lips!

It all came to an end in 1380, with the Chioggia War: Venice risked defeat and could by no means do without Poveglia and its strategic position: a year beforehand, the defensive octagon was built that we can still see today. Local inhabitants were exempted from military service and therefore were not obliged to provide any help: the entire population of the island was transferred to Giudecca and Poveglia was converted into a fortress.

Thereafter to the end of the 1700s, the island was only an important defensive node. In 1661, the descendants of the old residents were offered the possibility of settling again on the island – but the Serene Republic received a rebuke: yet further proof of the poor patriotism of the people of Poveglia. By 1777, the two "lazzaretti" already active in the lagoon were close to collapse and Poveglia was chosen as the site for the "Lazzaretto Novissimo", used to quarantine goods and crews from areas at risk of epidemics. The island retained this function until the early 1900s, when the buildings erected by the French and Austrians were converted into a long-term old people's home. This function also came to an end in 1968 and the island was abandoned to vandals, rodents and weeds. Today, however, Poveglia is enjoying a new renaissance: CTS (Student Tourist Centre) has presented a project for the restoration and revitalisation of the island approved by Venice City Council with the patronage of UNESCO.

Poveglia: *the island owes its name to the numerous poplars growing here; its Latin name was Popilia. Abandoned in 1968, its renaissance is linked with an ambitious and recently approved re-qualification project.*

The buildings will be renovated in full respect of their original features and will host up to 200 students having the chance to attend conventions, films, concerts and art performances. One of the buildings will be used exclusively for temporary exhibitions, while another will host a museum dedicated to the history, culture and nature of the lagoon.

The north area will be cultivated with organic agriculture methods and greenhouses will also be installed for protected crops – while the octagon will house a museum detailing the defensive structures installed in the lagoon. The island will also see the creation of a lagoon park characterised by paths for pedestrians and cyclists, as well as points of observation of flora and fauna. The project also includes a natural aquarium to admire and study the behaviour of native fish, lagoon vegetation and water-birds ensuring complete respect of Nature.

Sacca Sessola

This large island is man-made: it was created in 1870 as a land-fill exploiting an existing inlet – a kind of marine waste tip where the sludge dragged from the city canals or building demolition waste could be deposited. It was named Sessola because its outline recalls the bucket used in Venice to remove water from the base of boats. Its particular geographical location ensured an enviable microclimate, so much so that it was initially used to grow vegetables and tall trees, including palms. In 1911, Italy was struck by a violent cholera epidemic and the island was converted from a kind of out-of-town Eden into a contagious disease hospitalisation area.

Its special climate saw it chosen in 1931 as the home for a modern hospital treating tuberculosis: the central building for all medical work – a prototype of modern hospital blocks – was surrounded by 19 other buildings for collateral activities, even including a cinema. The centre was inaugurated in 1936 and at the time was considered to be one of the most avant-garde in Europe. The agricultural vocation was never abandoned – in fact, it was exploited to make the area entirely self-sufficient: the olive trees planted all around the centre produced table oil for patients and livestock were also reared. The sanatorium was closed in 1979, with all the consequent deterioration caused by such abandon of the island. Various and often contrary renovation projects were proposed but in the end an exclusive luxury resort was set up – which is still waiting to be inaugurated.

Once home to a psychiatric hospital, today the island of San Clemente is home to a luxury hotel. Background, Giudecca, with the incomparable profile of the Redentore Church.

San Clemente

It was initially a staging-post for pilgrims travelling to the Holy Land, that the Augustinian monks converted into a convent in 1160 and then abandoned in the 1400s. Thereafter, the island was used by the Serene Republic to offer initial hospitality to dignitaries and illustrious guests.

In the 1500s, San Clemente became a luxury "lazzaretto" colony for important personages from places hit by the plague and it was precisely from here in 1630 that the pestilence spread to Venice and then to the hinterland – at least, this is what tradition claims: it is said that Marquis De Stirgis, the Ambassador of the Duke of Mantua, infected a poor carpenter who unknowingly returned to the city taking death with him. In 1645, it was acquired by Andrea Mocenigo and then settled by the Camaldolite Friars.

The monks departed in 1810 and after a short period as a military site, in 1855 the Austrians demolished the convent and set up a female asylum. This psychiatric hospital later accepted male patients and was only closed in 1992. Following careful restoration, the entire island is now home to a luxury hotel complex.

San Clemente: *the delightful 1600s facade of the Church of San Clemente.*

San Erasmo & Vignole

When the inhabitants of Altino moved into the lagoon, the two islands were considered as the "vegetable garden" of Venice, so much so that even today the landscape is characterised by few farmhouses set amidst extensive fields. Wine was once the main product, as evidently recalled in the name of the island – Vignole – but today is rather limited. San Erasmo in any case still celebrates on the first Sunday of October the Wine Must Festival: new wine can be enjoyed, accompanied by "sugoli", and market garden produce is on sale at the exhibition-market set up for the occasion (local artichokes, asparagus and cardoons are justly famous). The island also boasts a small village with about 800 inhabitants in all, while Vignole has only around fifty. The two islands were already settled in Roman times: Martial wrote about the wealthy Altino people who built their country villas here. Today, no traces remain: in fact, once Venice became the centre of power, most of the population left the surrounding islands to set up their homes in the new city, exploiting their former palaces as quarries for construction materials. There are two monuments worthy of note: San Erasmo has the so-called Massimiliana Tower and Vignole the Sant'Andrea Fort. Standing at the south-western tip of the island, the Tower is a circular fortress designed by the French but built by the Austrians in the first half of the 1800s; it was originally surrounded by water but today, on the other hand, by a vegetable garden. It was named after Maximillian, the brother of Hapsburg Emperor Franz Joseph, who succeeded Radetzky as the Lombard-Veneto governor and sought refuge here during an insurrection. It was recently restored as a site for exhibitions and cultural events. The Sant'Andrea Fort, on the other hand, was built in Vignole in the 1500s by Michele Sanmicheli, a famous military architect from Verona who worked for the Serene Republic. Together with the castle at San Nicolò del Lido, it stood guard over the entrances to the port. The design of this fort aroused the jealousy of Sanmicheli's colleagues, as narrated by Giorgio Vasari in his *Lives*: gossip claimed that if the forty-two canons installed in the fort were fired at the same time, the building would have collapsed – saying farewell to defence against the enemy! The Senate decided to test the structure, filled it with artillery and ordered simultaneous firing. The noise and smoke were astonishing but the fort suffered no damage – so much so

The laurel cloisters on the island of San Giorgio, now home to the Cini Foundation.

The abbey complex of San Giorgio Maggiore.

that in 1797 the only canon shots fired by the Republic of St. Mark against the French came precisely from here: Napoleon's ship *Le Liberateur d'Italie* attempted to force the port blockade; it was hit, captured and its captain died during the action.

 San Francesco del Deserto

This tiny island owes its name to a legendary episode in the life of the Saint: in 1220, the ship carrying him back to Italy from his travels in Syria was struck by a storm and sought refuge at the island. Here, St. Francis struck his pine staff into the earth and it immediately took root. Today, this staff has grown into a tree and the Minor Friars living in the convent are always delighted to show it to tourists. Over and above the legend, in 1233 Jacopo Michiel, the owner of the island, commissioned a small church which he donated to the Franciscans. The convent was abandoned in 1420 because of the risk of malaria – the result, as for many other islands, of erosion by the rivers flowing out into the northern part of the lagoon and consequent swamping. The Minor Friars returned here thirty years later and since then only

left the site during the suppression in the Napoleonic period. With San Lazzaro and San Giorgio Maggiore, it is one of the last hermitages remaining in the lagoon – and is the place where original peace and quiet is still best preserved, since there are no public services: visitors have to hire a boat in Burano or directly telephone the friars to be picked up.

 ## San Giorgio in Alga

The Benedectines founded a convent here in XI century, dedicating the adjacent church to St. George, hence the name of the island:. "Alga" was added later, on becoming a characteristic of the site because of the effects of the River Brenta and its nearby estuary. The Benedictine monastery also enjoyed some importance even outside the territories of the Serene Republic, so much so that in 1328 Mastino della Scala, the Lord of Verona, married Taddea da Carrara here. Its vicinity to the Paduan hinterland, the River Brenta and the Fusina channel for centuries meant it was an almost obligatory staging-post for anyone arriving in Venice from the southeast and this is why it was often home to arrivals and departures during official visits by European monarchs. Mention must be made in this regard of the magnificent ceremony organised for the departure of Henry III, King of France, in 1574. In 1715, a fire destroyed the entire complex, including its impressive library; it was then turned into a prison for political prisoners and, on the arrival of the French, was converted into a fortress defending the city, complete with a powderhouse. The island was used for military purposes until the end of the Second World War – since then, it has remained completely abandoned: as the perimeter wall progressively collapses, vegetation and mice inside do their worst. The few ancient remains left intact after the fire were stolen and in the 1980s the so-called "Brenta Mafia" criminal organisation turned it into a hiding place. In 2001, the Venetian Curia – the owner of the island – engaged a cultural association to raise funds for its restoration and to set up a Lagoon Environment Study Centre.

 ## San Giorgio Maggiore

In the Middle Ages, this small island was known as the "island of cypress trees" and was owned by the ruling family. In 982, doge Tribuno Memmo donated it to the Benedectines so that an abbey could be built. At the time, the island boasted numerous salt fields, several mills and a small church dedicated to St. George. The Benedectines brought here

Front View of the church of San Giorgio.

the mortal remains of St. Stephen, to whom the tiny church was also dedicated, and over the years the monastery acquired bequests and donations that allowed it to expand its properties and the abbot to extend his power.

The Serene Republic also used it as a luxury residence for important guests: particular mention can be made of stays by Frederick II in 1232 and Cosimo de' Medici in 1433, exiled to Venice after he was ousted from Florence. The church, convent and annex buildings were involved in numerous projects through to the definitive, monumental complex we can still admire today, largely the work of Andrea Palladio and Baldassare Longhena. The Benedictine order enjoyed very strong bonds with the Serene Republic, so much so that the territories around the Venetian lagoon and many of its islands boasted a great many monasteries and coenoby. The monks offered peasants and fishermen an example of a simple life, based not only on prayer but also on work; they promised genuine faith, in keeping with their own hard-working existence, and in the end ensured peace where other places suffered from endemic revolts.

With the arrival of the French in 1797, the monastery was suppressed – yet when Venice was returned to the Austrians, the empire restored the abbot, to the extent that in 1800 the abbey hosted the conclave that elected Pope Pius VII (Rome was then in the hands of the French, who had proclaimed the Republic). In 1806, following the annexation of Venice into the Cisalpine Republic, the monastery was definitively suppressed and became home to the Customs Offices and

San Lazzaro degli Armeni: *the convent for centuries was the only cultural link between Europe and Armenia. Abandoned in the 1500s, the island came to life again in 1717 thanks to Armenian monk Manug di Pietro, a refugee from the Peloponnesus after the Turkish conquest.*

the Artillery Command. Only the church was retained as a place of worship. All kinds of spoliation followed, reducing the complex to a mere shell. The end of the 1700s saw the removal of the huge canvas with *The Caan Wedding* painted by Il Veronese for the refectory of the convent. It was taken to Paris to enhance the Louvre Gallery - where it is still housed today. In 1951, Count Vittorio Cini acquired most of the Abbey complex, to turn it into the head offices of the foundation dedicated to the memory of his son, Giorgio. The buildings were renovated and the interiors embellished with works from suppressed convents. Today, the island is a renowned education and cultural centre.

San Lazzaro degli Armeni

This tiny island is opposite the Lido and its oriental "onion" bell tower ensures an incomparable profile. At the end of XII century, a small church and a hospital were built here, which later became a leper colony (hence the place-name dedicated to St. Lazarus, the patron saint of leprosy sufferers). In the 1500s, the island was completely abandoned and its renaissance was the work of an Armenian monk, Manug di Pietro, known as Mechitar. He arrived in Venice in 1715, fleeing from Methoni, in the Peloponnesus, which has fallen into the hands of the Turks. In 1717, he managed to obtain San Lazzaro from the Serene Republic and built here a monastery complex – to his own design – that is still active today. It was unharmed even during the Napoleonic suppressions: given their origins, the Armenian Fathers raised the Turkish flag and the island was initially considered untouchable. Later, once the trick was discovered, the new owners in any case considered the community as an important cultural rather than religious centre, and in 1810 Napoleon issued a decree that confirmed the conservation of the convent. Today, the complex is open to visitors and there are facilities for guests seeking to rediscover the atmospheres that fascinated Lord Byron, who stayed here on several occasions. The large and precious library boasts an impressive collection of Armenian manuscripts and miniatures; although printing has long ceased, it was for centuries the main link between European culture and the Armenian world. The most curious and out of place object that visitors can admire here is the mummy of Prince Nehmekhet, the only Egyptian relic in the lagoon. zio in laguna.

The cloisters of San Michele Arcangelo.

San Michele & Sant'Ariano

San Michele and Sant'Ariano are today very different but once shared a common destiny: they were both home to monasteries and were both later converted into cemeteries. The island today known as San Michele until 1835 was split in two by a canal: one part was called *Cavana de Muran*, because it offered shelter to boats on the route between Venice and Murano; the other was named San Cristoforo della Pace (St. Christopher of Peace) and was home to a convent. It seems that in x century *Cavana* was already home to a small church dedicated to St. Michael Archangel, while it is certain that the tiny island was granted in 1212 by the Serene Republic to three Camaldolite monks, who founded a monastery here.

With time, the place even became an Abbey and its library was an important meeting place for geographers and explorers. The friars in short had gathered an impressive collection of travel books, pilots' charts and maps of the entire world.

It was here that Friar Mauro in the 1400s created his famous map of the world, which revolutionised the cosmography of the period. Today, it is in the Marciana Library, while the collection of books found refuge in Rome together with the Camoldolites, when the convent was suppressed in 1810. The Austrians then turned the island into a penitentiary, where Silvio Pellico and

Pietro Maroncelli were imprisoned 1819-1822 before being transferred to Spielberg. in 1829, the island and convent were granted to the Reformed Franciscans, who still today look after the magnificent Renaissance church designed by Mauro Codussi in 1469. San Cristoforo island, on the other hand, was converted in 1807 by the French into a cemetery, who also in Venice applied the Napoleonic health rule whereby burial places had to be well away from the city. By 1835, this tiny island had become too small for the purpose so that the canal separating it from San Michele was filled in and even the old *Cavana de Muran* became a cemetery. Even then, public works were notoriously slow – so much so that the official inauguration of the new cemetery only took place in 1876.

Sant'Ariano was once part of the larger island of Costanziaco, which later disappeared because of the erosion effects of lagoon currents – a fate shared by many other islands in the northern lagoon.

A Benedictine monastery was built here in the 1200s, whose origin is very curious: the Giustinian noble family had no male heirs and to prevent extinction the Pope allowed the last descendant, Nicolò, to leave the Benedictine Order and marry. His chosen bride was Margherita, daughter of Doge Vitale II Michiel: it was a kind of atonement, since many Giustinians died during a disastrous expedition against the Turks, promoted by the doge himself, who was lynched shortly after in the wake of this failure.

The marriage bore five sons, whereupon Nicolò decided that he had done his duty and could return to the convent. The marriage evidently involved great sacrifices for the couple, since his wife also abandoned secular life to found a monastery at Sant'Ariano that later became a refuge (perhaps even a prison) for numerous Venetian noblewomen. The convent was abandoned in 1439 because of the unhealthy conditions of the place, following swamping in this part of the lagoon.

Its suppression was also the outcome of the laxity of the novices, a common aspect in many other nunneries on the islands.

It was said that the nobility often made nocturnal visits for purposes not entirely in keeping with prayer and mortification of the flesh. The Serene Republic therefore decreed that the island should become the ossarium of the city – a function it retained until 1933. A wall was built in the 1600s all around its perimeter – still standing today – to prevent seafarers seeing the piles of skulls and bones whitening in the Sun.

Today, Sant'Ariano is the realm of snakes – *carbonassi* in Venetian dialect – so that it is one of the few islands not infested by rats and mice.

San Secondo

This is the first island seen when crossing the Bridge of Liberty towards Venice. Today, it is buried under vegetation but it was once home to a convent of Benedictine nuns where the remains of San Secondo were preserved. The holy reliquaries arrived from Asti in the 1200s: Pietro Tiepolo, after conquering the city, purchased them with the intention of placing them in the Church of San Geremia. A sudden storm surprised the ship carrying them from Mestre to Venice, forcing the sailors to seek refuge on this tiny island. The crew raised the sails again when calm returned – only for a new storm to break and prevent the ship leaving the tiny port. It seemed as if San Secondo himself wanted to remain here – and his wish was granted: his body, still intact after a millennium, was placed in the monastery. In 1569, following a fire that almost destroyed the Arsenal and threatened to involve the entire city of Venice, the Serene Republic decreed that munitions should be stocked on the smaller islands and such a depot was built even on San Secondo. In 1824, the church and the monastery were demolished and the remains of the Saint were transferred to the Gesuati Temple – this time without the interference of storms. During the insurrection against the Austrians in 1848, the Imperial artillery hit the powder-house and the island was then abandoned.

San Servolo

San Servolo shares with San Clemente the destiny of having been home to an asylum, founded in 1715 and closed in 1980. However, the island boasts a much longer history, lost in the dark centuries of the barbarian invasions: the Benedectines of Santo Stefano di Altino sought refuge from the Franks here and founded the most ancient monastery of the lagoon. At the time, it was actually ten times smaller than the present-day island – which says a great deal about the Venetian "hunger" for land and the need to enlarge tiny islands to meet the needs of a capital. In 998 a secret meeting took place here between the doge, Pietro II Orseolo, and Ottone II. The emperor had been ousted from Rome but, before giving up his dream of re-founding the Roman Empire, asked

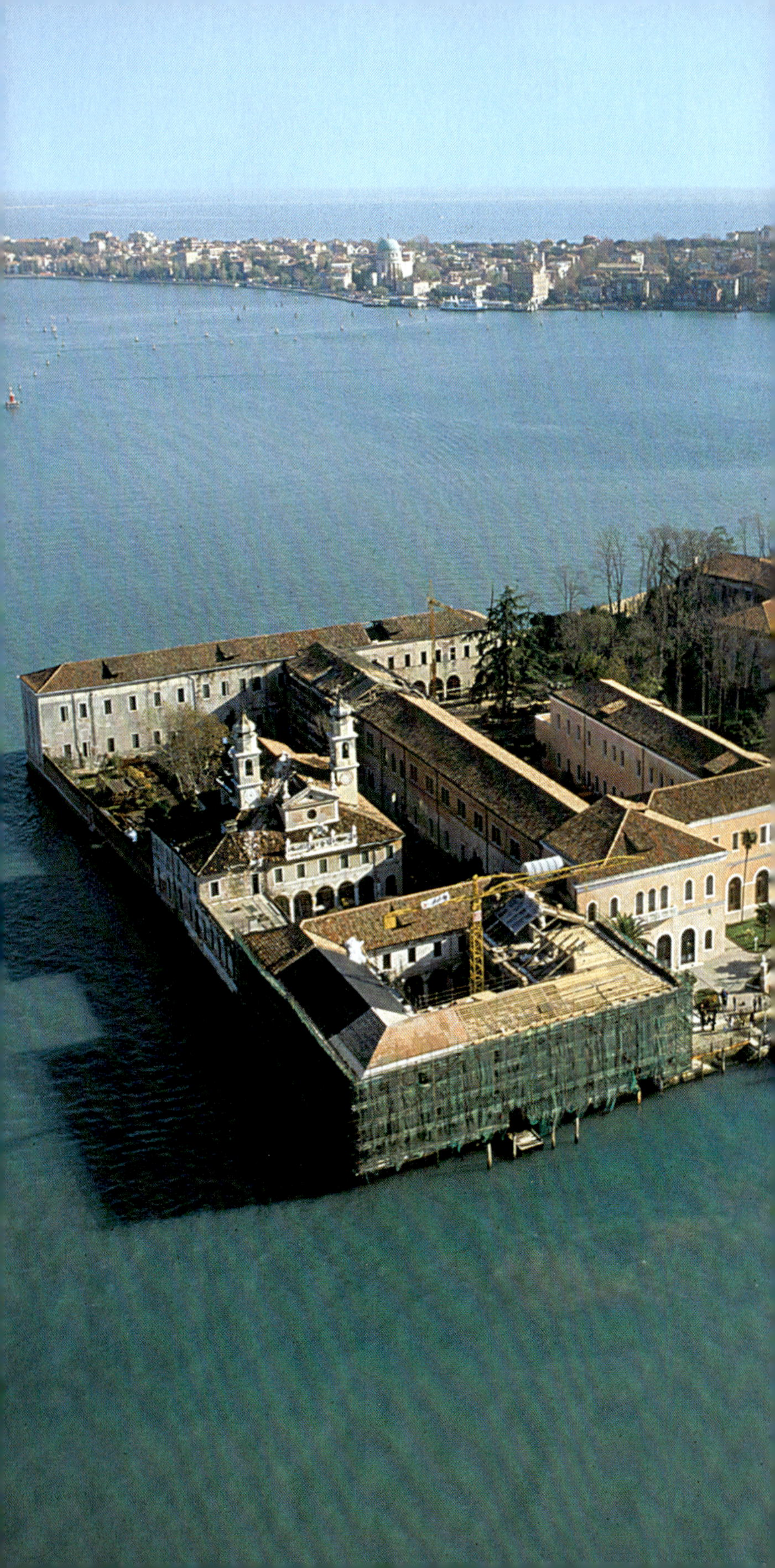

San Servolo: *the imposing buildings characterising the island were built as an asylum for high-born mental illness patients. In 1997, the island became home to Venice International University.*

The ruins of Santo Spirito island, abandoned since 1918.

Venice and its fleet for aid, only to receive a clear refusal. In the 1200s, the nuns of the same order took over from the Benedectines; as in other nunneries in the lagoon, laxity was also common here and in 1615 the young nuns were all transferred to the Jesuit convent in Venice, then unused following the expulsion of the Jesuits from the territories of the Serene Republic. The Hospitaler Fathers arrived a century later and founded a hospital for the war-wounded. Between 1733 and 1766, a mental asylum was built exclusively for the noble families (lower class sufferers became vagabonds or were sent to prison), but the arrival of the French saw an end to such "social distinctions" and the site was opened to sufferers of any condition. In 1997, the Institute was converted into the head offices of the *Venice International University* and today this former mental home welcomes students from all over the world.

Sant'Angelo della Polvere

This tiny island today retains no signs of its past but for centuries was home to convents – and hides one of the many "spicy" stories involving the lagoon nuns, with an entertaining final variation. In 1474, the wives of the fishermen and farmers of Pellestrina and Malamocco sent an official protest to the Serene Republic: their husbands always returned from the Rialto market with half the money they should have earned. An inquiry was opened and it was discovered that the men stopped off at the convent to "relax" with the nuns. The good sisters, when the boats sailed past, displayed their own "wares" from the perimeter wall and the fishermen were unable to resist such temptations. In exchange for their attentions, the young nuns accepted only money, fish or vegetables. The ecclesiastic hierarchy ordered the immediate closure of the convent – yet the priests and magistrates sent to carry out these orders did not receive the same "warm welcome" reserved to the men of Pellestrina and Malamocco: the nuns threw such a hailstorm of stones from the parapets of the convent that the bailiffs were forced to retreat! Only the navy and soldiers finally managed to evict them. The nuns were then transferred to the Santa Croce Convent at Giudecca, which was easier to supervise, and their place was taken by the Carmelites. In the mid-1500s, the Senate turned the island into a gunpowder depot – hence its present-day name: it was first known as Sant'Angelo della Concordia. A bolt of lightning in 1689 struck the gunpowder depot, causing an explosion that destroyed almost all the buildings. Barracks were built here at the end of the 1700s – that were also used by the French – and the island remained a military site until the mid-1900s.

Today it is abandoned – the only visible relics are the concrete skeletons of two buildings and a rainwater tank built after the Second World War. Such a depressing end, that it would perhaps be better to invite the return of the merry nuns…

Santo Spirito

The first information indicating settlement on the island dates back to 1140, when the Augustinian Fathers built a monastery here, together with a small church and a hospital. After three centuries, the island was taken over by the Augustinian Hermits, who commissioned Sansovino to build a larger church, embellished with canvases by Titian and Palma il Vecchio. In this period, the island was popular with nobles and international dignitaries, who stopped here before proceeding to Venice. Emperor Frederick III stayed here for one night in 1468; the following day, he was welcomed aboard "Bucentaur" by the doge in person and was escorted to the city by a numerous and lively naval procession. In 1656, the Pope ordered the suppression of the order; the furnishings and works of art were then taken to the new Salute Church. Twenty years or so later, the Minor Observant Friars fleeing from Candia following the Turkish invasion occupied this island and installed the precious library and numerous reliquaries they had managed to save. In 1806, however, the Napoleonic government decreed the suppression of convent, converting Santo Spirito to the military functions that continued until the Great War. Various old buildings were demolished and replaced by barracks, a prison and a powderhouse. In 1918, the island was abandoned and utterly neg-

The church of Santa Fosca in Torcello, built XII century.

lected: perimeter walls and buildings in hazardous condition or already collapsed, weeds everywhere. As if this were not enough, smugglers using the island in the 1950s as a depot for their goods caused a fire that destroyed the church. Since then, it has seen only plunder and pillage.

Torcello

Once home to a Bishop and a centre of considerable importance, today Torcello is a semi-deserted island still dominated by the elegant profiles of the Church of Santa Fosca and the ancient Cathedral of Santa Maria Assunta. The former dates back to XII century, while an ancient inscription indicates 639 A.D. as the foundation date for the latter, during the governance of Isacio, the Exarch of Ravenna who then also had jurisdiction over the Venetian lagoon. Growing barbarian threats saw the population of Altino progressively move to the islands, and in that year even the Bishop decided to move to the lagoon. The island was for centuries a kind of second capital, with about twenty thousand inhabitants, and enjoyed exclusive control of wool processing until the early 1300s. Even before the area became a swamp, it was decided in the middle of VIII century to transfer the home of the Doge to the Rialto islands – modern Venice – and this caused the slow decline of Torcello: despite remaining an important centre for many centuries, its population began to shrink and the island became a kind of quarry for the new capital. Roman remains and Byzantine monuments were soon looted to decorate Venetian palaces. In 1689, the bishop's see was finally transferred – in any case, the Bishop had resided in Murano since the 1400s: as well as suffering the competition of Venice, as of XII century Torcello became increasingly swampy and its population had dwindled. Special mention must also be made of the Devil's Bridge which, like all original Venetian bridges, has no parapets. It is linked with an infernal legend. During the Austrian occupation, a young noblewoman fell in love with a young Hapsburg officer; her family opposed their marriage, considering it to be an act of submission to the invader; the young lady was sent away from the city and her lover was assassinated. The young girl fell into such deep despair that a friend of the family, an expert in magical arts, offered to help her. He sought a witch able to bring the young man back to life and finally found the right person: Ester, a Jewish sorceress. She sought a powerful demon and made a pact with him: if the young officer came to life again, Ester would have given this demon the souls of seven Christian children. The devil accepted and the meeting was set for Christmas Eve on the bridge in Torcello. Ester and the young girl arrived for the appointment by gondola; the sorceress marked the steps of the bridge with certain signs – the devil immediately appeared and threw into the water one of the three keys of Time held in his mouth. The young Austrian then materialised, the young lady crossed the bridge, the two embraced and then disappeared. Ester kept her appointment with the demon for seven nights afterwards to consign the souls of the seven children yet was unable to keep her promise: during one of her rituals, she made a mistake and flew up into the air. The devil turned up for the appointment that year and for many years afterwards but then became bored and sent an emissary in his place. Still today, anyone strolling near the bridge on Christmas Eve might well see a black cat sitting on the steps, waiting …

Contents

Burano 5
Certosa 8
I Lazzaretti 8
Il Lido 12
La Giudecca 13
La Grazia 15
Mazzorbo 16
Murano 17
Poveglia 21
Sacca Sessola 24
San Clemente 25
San Erasmo & Vignole 28
San Francesco del Deserto 30
San Giorgio in Alga 32
San Giorgio Maggiore 32
San Lazzaro degli Armeni 36
San Michele & Sant'Ariano 37
San Secondo 39
San Servolo 39
Sant'Angelo della Polvere 43
Santo Spirito 44
Torcello 45

All our books are produced entirely in Italy using papers from specifically dedicated forestry operations with regular replanting.
Moreover, all materials used are ecology-compatible in full respect of the environment and people.
All our production is based on full respect of regulations concerning safety, consumer health and our workers.

Printed in January 2009
by EBS Editoriale Bortolazzi-Stei
San Giovanni Lupatoto (Verona)
Italy